Featherstone

fantastic ideas for
ce   vals

ALISTAIR BRYCE-CLEGG

Featherstone
An imprint of Bloomsbury Publishing Plc

50 Bedford Square
London
WC1B 3DP
UK

1385 Broadway
New York
NY 10018
USA

www.bloomsbury.com

Bloomsbury is a registered trademark of Bloomsbury Publishing Plc

First published 2015

British Library Cataloguing-in-Publication Data
A catalogue record for this book is available from the British Library.

ISBN:
PB 978-1-4729-1327-2
ePDF 978-1-4729-2426-1

Library of Congress Cataloging-in-Publication Data
A catalogue record for this book is available from the Library of Congress.

10 9 8 7 6 5 4 3 2 1

Printed and bound in India by Replika Press Pvt. Ltd.

This book is produced using paper that is made from wood grown in managed, sustainable
forests. It is natural, renewable and recyclable. The logging and manufacturing processes
conform to the environmental regulations of the country of origin.

To view more of our titles please visit www.bloomsbury.com

Contents

Introduction

A young child's concept of the passing of time is often punctuated with key memories of exciting times, such as celebrations and festivals with family members and friends. It is important that children not only enjoy celebrations and festivals that are significant to them and their culture, but that they also experience and understand the celebrations and festivals of others.

This book is packed with activities that link to many - but not all - of the key celebrations and festivals that are relevant to the children in your setting.

All of the activities have been tried and tested on real children and all have resulted in high levels of engagement.

As well as being stand-alone activities, the skills and ideas can be transferred into other experiences, to capture a child's interest both within and beyond the theme of the book.

So whether you are making snowman slime or creating fireworks in a bottle - let your imagination and the children's interests take these activity ideas off the page and into play!

Food allergy alert

FOOD allergy!

When using food stuffs to enhance your play opportunities, always be mindful of potential food allergies. Look out for this symbol on the relevant pages.

Skin allergy alert

SKIN allergy!

Some detergents and soaps can cause skin reactions. Always be aware of potential skin allergies when letting children mix anything with their hands, and always provide facilities to wash materials off after they have been in contact with skin. Watch out for this symbol on the relevant pages.

Safety issues

Social development can only take place when children are given opportunities to experiment and take reasonable risks in a safe environment. Encouraging independence and the use of natural resources inevitably raises some health and safety issues; these are identified where appropriate.

Children need help and good models for washing their hands when using natural materials or preparing food. They may need reminding not to put things in their mouths, and to be extra careful with real-life or found resources.

SAFETY FiRST!

Coloured salt patterns

What you need:

- **Table salt** (a large bag)
- **Bowls or freezer bags**
- **Paint or food colouring**
- **Spoon**
- **Flat surface** (for drying)
- **Light box, or tin foil, or paper**
- **Diwali patterns as examples** (printouts or pages in a book)

Taking it forward

- Make a display that includes other Diwali resources such as lanterns, fabric or pictures.
- Use rice instead of salt for a different texture – or try using both.

What to do:

1. Divide the salt into bowls or bags.
2. Add a few drops of food colouring or paint to each bowl or bag (start with a small amount – it is easy to add more!)
3. Stir the contents of the bowl or shake the bag (make sure it is tightly fastened), until all of the salt is coated in the colouring.
4. Pour the salt onto a flat surface and leave to dry.
5. Once dry, use the salt to create beautiful Diwali patterns on a light box, sheet of tin foil, or some paper.
6. Try creating rings of colour then ask the children to use their fingertips to gently push the salt into patterns. (See image below for inspiration!)

What's in it for the children?

The process of colouring salt is always a fascinating one for the children. They will learn more about the festival of Diwali, whilst improving their fine motor ability.

Hand biscuits

What you need:

- Card
- Felt-tip pen
- Scissors
- Pre-bought biscuit dough or biscuit dough made from a recipe
- Rolling pin
- Knife
- Baking paper
- Baking tray
- Access to an oven
- Icing tubes
- Henna and Rangoli patterns as examples (printouts or pages in a book)

What to do:

1. Draw around a child's hand onto card and then carefully cut it out to create a template.

2. Roll out the biscuit dough to around half a centimetre thick.

3. Place the hand template onto the dough and use a knife to cut around it.

4. Line a baking tray with baking paper.

5. Transfer the biscuits to the tray and bake for the required amount of time (see package instructions or recipe).

6. Once cooked and cooled, encourage the children to make traditional Henna patterns on their biscuit hands, using the icing tubes.

7. Eat!

Taking it forward

- Invite someone into your setting to show the children how Henna patterns are created on real hands.

What's in it for the children?

The children will see how materials change state through the baking process, as well as celebrating the traditions of other cultures.

Doily Rangoli pattern fireworks

What you need:

- Black, dark blue or white sugar paper
- Metallic paint and/or glitter paint
- Paint tray
- Selection of doilies
- Sponges

What to do:

1. Place the sheets of sugar paper on a flat surface.
2. Decant the paints into a tray.
3. Place the doilies on the sugar paper in a decorative arrangement.
4. Use the sponge to apply paint to the entire doily.
5. Make sure that the paint gets into all the gaps in the pattern.
6. Carefully peel back the doily to reveal a Rangoli firework pattern.
7. Leave to dry.

Taking it forward

- Experiment with different types of paint for a range of effects.
- Place glitter or sequins on the pattern whilst the paint is still wet for additional texture and sparkle!

What's in it for the children?

There are plenty of opportunities for the children to talk about the patterns in the doilies, and also to make a pattern by painting through the gaps of a stencil.

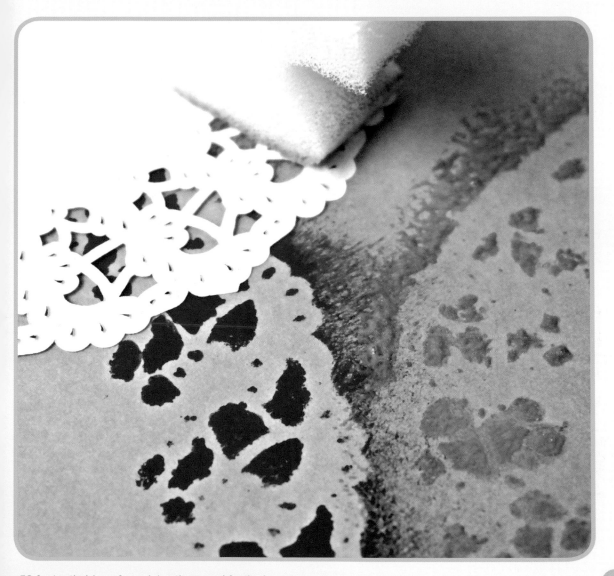

Stars in a jar

What you need:

- Tin foil
- Ruler
- Scissors
- Jam jars
- Soft surface (such as a carpet tile)
- Cocktail stick
- Tea lights
- Lighter or matches

What to do:

1. Measure and cut a strip of tin foil that is the same height and circumference as your jam jar.
2. Lay the tin foil flat on a soft surface.
3. Use the cocktail stick to prick the tin foil over its entire surface.
4. Loosely roll the tin foil and place it around the outside of the jar.
5. Drop a tea light into the jar.
6. Light the tea light (adult only), turn out the lights and watch the twinkle of the stars in a jar!

Taking it forward

- Make several jars to create a starry night display – or for a more impressive display try making this on a much larger scale, using a glass vase or a storm lantern.

What's in it for the children?

The pricking of the foil encourages fine motor dexterity. The children can also make a comparison between the starry night sky and what they have created.

✚ Health & Safety

Elements of this activity are adult only tasks. Always carry out risk assessments when using fire.

Glowing lantern

What you need:

- Measuring tape
- Small foil pie cases or jam jar lids
- Baking parchment
- Scissors
- Wax crayons
- Glue
- Tea lights
- Lighter or matches

What to do:

1. Measure the circumference of the foil pie case or lid.
2. Cut a piece of baking parchment the length of the pie case measurement.
3. Spend some time decorating the baking parchment with a picture or simple pattern.
4. Wrap the baking parchment around the outside of the pie case or lid, to form a tube.
5. Blob glue on the edges of the baking parchment and stick together to secure the tube.
6. Place a tea light onto the pie dish or lid inside the baking parchment tube.
7. Light the tea light (adult only) and watch the artwork glow!

Taking it forward

- Make a big collaborative version using a larger floor candle.
- It may be easier for less confident children to wrap the baking parchment around a jam jar, and then place the tea light inside.

What's in it for the children?

The children will learn how to record and explore patterns and stories related to Diwali, as well as creating a lantern, which is symbolic of the festival.

Health & Safety

Elements of this activity are adult only tasks. Always carry out risk assessments when using fire.

Fireworks in a bottle

What you need:

- ¼ litre of cooking oil
- 1 litre plastic bottle
- ½ litre water
- Various food colourings
- Glitter and/or sequins
- Alka Seltzer

What to do:

1. Pour the oil into the plastic bottle.
2. Add the water.
3. Drop some food colouring into the bottle.
4. Add the glitter or sequins.
5. Securely fasten the bottle lid, and then shake well.
6. Remove the lid and quickly crumble some Alka Seltzer into the bottle.
7. Stand back and watch the display!

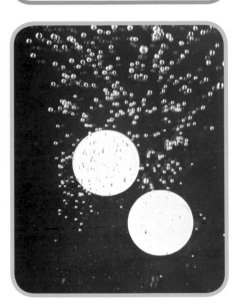

Taking it forward

- For a team display create a number of different sized bottles to use together.
- Try this activity in a dark space and shine torches on the moving colours and sequins once the bottles have been shaken.

What's in it for the children?

The children can investigate what happens when they mix oil and water together, not to mention the reflection of light from the glitter and sequins, and the explosive addition of the Alka Seltzer!

Glow stick balloon ghosts

What you need:

- Glow sticks
- White balloons
- Balloon pump
- **Black permanent marker** (or paper, glue and scissors)

What to do:

1. Activate a glow stick.
2. Push it into the neck of a balloon.
3. Use the balloon pump to blow up the balloon and tie the end in a knot.
4. Draw a face onto the balloon with the permanent marker, or cut a face out of paper and stick it on.
5. Enjoy!

Taking it forward

- Group a few 'ghosts' together for a really spooky experience!
- Use the 'ghosts' as a stimulus for mark making or writing.
- Let the children move the 'ghosts' around your setting and see where they glow the brightest.

What's in it for the children?

The children will develop some tricky dexterity skills when they draw on a balloon with a marker!

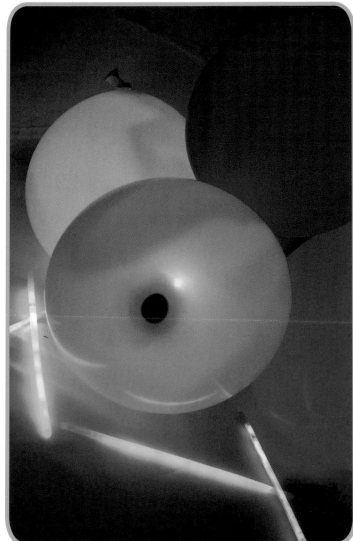

Cotton bud skeleton

What you need:

- Black sugar paper
- Scissors
- White paint
- **Small bowl** (for the paint)
- Paintbrush or sponge
- Glue
- Cotton buds

What to do:

1. Cut the sugar paper so that it is big enough to fit the length of the children's forearm and hand.

2. Roll up the children's sleeves and cover with white paint one hand and the underside of the same arm (up to the elbow).

3. Ask the children to carefully place their arm and hand onto the sugar paper to create a white print. Take care that they do not smudge the print when they remove their arm from the paper.

4. Once the print is dry, brush it with a thin covering of glue.

5. While the glue is still wet, position the cotton buds to look like the bones in the arm and hand.

6. Leave to dry.

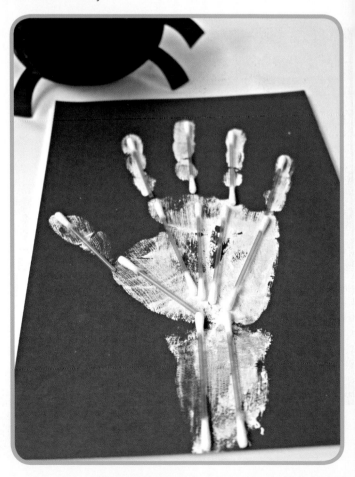

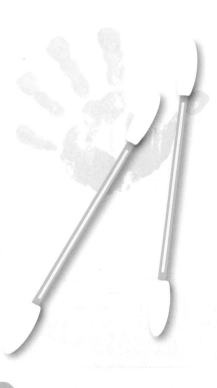

Taking it forward

- Use different parts of the body and the same process to create other prints, such as skeleton feet.

- Work as a team to create an entire mini skeleton using only cotton buds (see image below).

What's in it for the children?

There are lots of opportunities here for the children to learn and talk about their body, how it is made, and the important function of our skeleton.

Glowing ice hand

What you need:

- Rubber or surgical gloves
- **Tonic water** (with quinine – most tonic water does contain it, but it is worth checking)
- **Access to a freezer**
- **Scissors**
- **Black light**

What to do:

1. Hold the gloves open and carefully fill with tonic water.
2. Tie the end in a tight knot.
3. Put the glove in the freezer overnight.
4. The next day, take the glove out of the freezer and cut the end off, just below the tied knot.
5. Use the cut to peel the glove away from the ice hand (let the hand 'warm up' for a couple of minutes before the children try and peel off the glove).
6. In a dark space turn on the black light and watch the ice hands glow!

Taking it forward

- For an extra spooky effect try floating the ice hands in a water tray.
- Assist the children in partially filling some balloons with tonic water and then blowing them up in a dark space to give them a spooky glow!

What's in it for the children?

The children will observe how materials can change state, as the tonic water changes from a liquid to a solid. This is also a great activity for encouraging conversation, especially about why the hands have a mysterious glow.

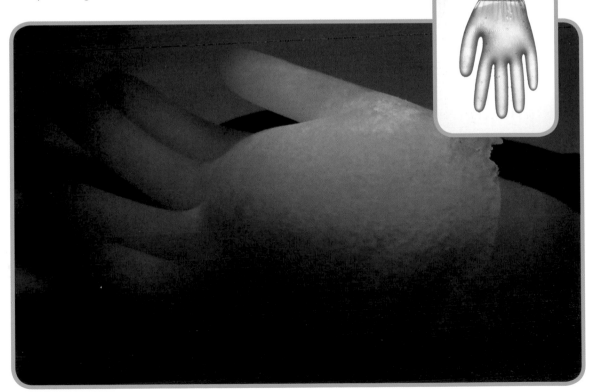

Pumpkin puffy paint

What you need:

- 1 small pumpkin
- Chopping board
- 1 chopping knife
- A pan partly filled with water
- Access to a hob
- Potato masher or food processor
- Spoon
- Orange food colouring
- 2 cups of PVA glue
- 2 cups of shaving foam (unscented)
- A large sheet of paper, or a flat surface

What to do:

1. Chop up the pumpkin and boil in a pan of water for about fifteen minutes, until soft (adult only).
2. Strain the boiled pumpkin then mash or purée until it is completely pulped and smooth.
3. Leave it to cool.
4. Add food colouring. The quantity depends on how bright the puffy paint is going to be!
5. Next, add the glue and stir well.
6. Slowly stir in the shaving foam (don't stir too much as this will make the paint less 'puffy'!)
7. Spoon or pour the paint out onto paper or a flat surface.
8. Either allow the children to play with it straight away, or leave the paint to 'set' for a few minutes before they get their fingers stuck in!

Taking it forward

- Save the pumpkin seeds to add a different texture to the puffy paint experience!

- Divide the mixture into separate pots and add a different colour to each pot. Try using the variety of colours to make a large puffy paint painting.

What's in it for the children?

This is a great activity for exploring texture - from the mashing of the pumpkin, to the puffiness of the paint.

 Health & Safety

Preparing and cooking the pumpkin is an adult only activity.

Glow-in-the-dark slime

What you need:

- 2 large mixing bowls
- Metal mixing spoon
- 2 cups of PVA glue
- 4 tablespoons glow-in-the dark paint
- **Neon food colouring** (optional – this makes the slime bright when it is not under a black light)
- ½ cup liquid starch or 1½ cups cornflour
- An additional 1 cup of PVA glue
- Black light torch or bulb

What to do:

1. Mix the glue, paint and food colouring together in a bowl.
2. Thoroughly mix the starch and additional PVA in a separate bowl.
3. Combine the glue mixture and the starch mixture and stir well.
4. Turn out the lights and switch on the black light to watch the slime glow!

SKIN allergy !

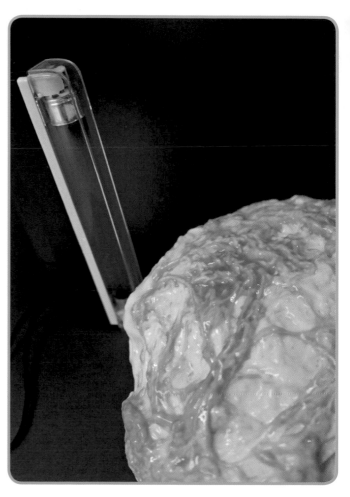

Taking it forward

- Why not make several different batches in different colours?
- Try adding plastic eyeballs or spiders to the slime to make it really spooky!

What's in it for the children?

The process of making the slime shows how different materials can change when they are mixed together. The slime itself is a great sensory experience.

Health & Safety

Make sure this is a closely supervised activity and a risk assessment is in place.

50 fantastic ideas for celebrations and festivals

Pumpkin crayon melt

What you need:

- **Crayons** (old or new)
- **Pumpkin**
- **Sticky dots or glue gun**
- **Hairdryer**

Taking it forward

- Try using several pumpkins in a variety of different sizes.
- Use the same technique on other fruit and vegetables to make a spooky vegetable patch.

➕ **Health & Safety**
Make sure that the children are carefully supervised around the hot glue and wax.

What to do:

1. Remove any paper covers from the crayons.
2. Use the glue gun to dab blobs of glue onto the top of the pumpkin.
3. Carefully stick the crayons into the hot glue.
4. Switch on the hairdryer and begin to gently heat the crayons.
5. As the crayons melt, move the hairdryer in different directions to make patterns with the dripping wax.

What's in it for the children?

The children will enjoy experimenting with colour, pattern and texture, as well as observing the effects that heat can have on different materials and their properties.

Shrunken apple heads

What you need:

- Apples
- Safety peeler
- Dough modelling tools
- Pips, seeds and black rice (optional)
- Wooden sticks or skewers

What to do:

1. Peel the apples with the safety peeler.

2. Use the dough modelling tools to carve some basic features into the apples (as the 'heads' will shrink, these can be quite exaggerated).

3. Push the pips, seeds or rice into the flesh of the apple - get creative to create extra features like teeth and hair.

4. Insert a stick into the bottom of the apple.

5. Leave to air-dry for about one week. Try not to let the apples touch during this stage.

Taking it forward

- Experiment with different tools to create a range of features on the apples.

- Different sizes and varieties of apple will give the children different results.

What's in it for the children?

This is a great way to observe decomposition, as well as investigating the rituals and customs of past civilizations and cultures. It is also a chance for the children to explore their creativity!

Exploding ghosts

What you need:

- Clear containers with lids
- Black marker (or a sticky label and pens)
- Cornflour
- Teaspoon
- Water
- Alka Seltzer

Taking it forward

- Create other container characters – how about an astronaut in a rocket, or a jumping kangaroo?
- Attach a photo of the child or their face to the container and let them send themselves up, up and away!

What to do:

1. On the outside of your container draw or stick a ghost face (the children will be putting them 'lid end down' to explode, so make sure the face will not be upside down!)
2. Put a teaspoon of cornflour in each container.
3. Fill to about two thirds full with water.
4. Put on the lid and give it a good shake to fully combine.
5. Take off the lid and drop in a piece of Alka Seltzer.
6. Quickly, put the lid back on and place the 'ghost' on the ground (lid side down).
7. Wait for the explosion…
8. …do it again!

What's in it for the children?

The children will experience cause and effect first hand, as well as enjoying an early introduction to science.

Chocolate finger sparklers

What you need:

- Cup
- Hot water
- Bowl
- Popping candy
- Hundreds and thousands
- Greaseproof paper
- Chocolate fingers

What to do:

1. Fill the cup with hot water (adult only).
2. Fill the bowl with a mixture of popping candy and hundreds and thousands.
3. Place a sheet of greaseproof paper onto a flat surface.
4. Dip the end of a chocolate finger into the hot water for a few seconds.
5. Remove the finger and put it straight into the bowl containing the hundreds and thousands and popping candy.
6. Turn the finger to make sure that the end is completely coated.
7. Remove from the bowl and leave to harden on the greaseproof paper.
8. Eat!

Taking it forward

- Try adding other sparkly additions to the chocolate fingers like edible glitter or silver balls.

What's in it for the children?

The chocolate melts in the hot water and then solidifies again as it is left to cool, which demonstrates the change in materials and their properties.

Firework fruit prints

What you need:

- **Citrus fruit** (e.g. grapefruit, orange, satsuma)
- **Knife**
- **Paint**
- **Tray**
- **Paper** (ideally absorbent paper such as sugar paper)
- **Glitter**

What to do:

1. Cut the citrus fruit in half at least one day before the activity, and leave uncovered to air-dry (this is the secret to getting a good print!)

2. Once the fruit has dried out, put a small amount of paint into the tray.

3. Dip the cut side of the citrus fruit into the paint and print directly onto the paper (absorbent paper will give the best print).

4. It may be helpful to have a separate piece of paper for a 'test' print. The segments of the citrus fruit should give the impression of an exploding firework.

5. While the paint is still wet, sprinkle with glitter.

6. Leave to dry.

Taking it forward

- Try using luminous or fluorescent paint.

- Mix powder paint with tonic water instead of plain water, and then use a black light to make the fireworks glow.

What's in it for the children?

This is a great activity for exploring texture, smell and colour. The citrus fruit smells great when it is first cut and feels wet. When the children come to use it to print with, it will look and feel very different.

Bonfire night gloop

What you need:

- Cornflour
- Water
- Mixing bowl
- Metal spoon
- Tray
- Food colouring
- Small bowls or plastic pots
- Cotton buds

What to do:

1. Mix the cornflour and water together to make gloop.
2. Pour the gloop into the bottom of a tray.
3. Put a small amount of food colouring into the small bowls or pots.
4. Dip the end of a cotton bud into the food colouring.
5. Place the end of the cotton bud into the gloop and watch the colour spread like an exploding firework.
6. Repeat until the tray is full of fireworks!

Taking it forward

- For bigger 'explosions' dip the corner of a baby wipe into the colouring and then place it on the gloop. Try dragging the baby wipe across the gloop for a different effect.
- Sprinkle glitter onto the gloop for even more sparkle!

What's in it for the children?

The children will enjoy experimenting with the unique solid and liquid properties of gloop. They can also observe how the food colouring spreads through the gloop and creates new colours as it mixes.

firework T-shirts

What you need:

- White T-shirt
- Paper
- Permanent markers in lots of colours
- Surgical spirit
- Iron or tumble dryer

What to do:

1. Put some paper inside the T-shirt to separate the front from the back.

2. Use the markers to make different sized dots all over the T-shirt.

3. Drip surgical spirit (adult only) onto the marker dots and watch the colours spread like fireworks.

4. Repeat until the children are happy with the effect.

5. Once dry, either iron with a hot iron or tumble-dry to seal the colour (adult only).

Taking it forward

- Experiment with different sized 'dots' and varied amounts of surgical spirit.

What's in it for the children?

This is an opportunity for the children to explore their creativity, engage in some colour mixing and see an example of cause, change and effect.

 Health & Safety

Handle the surgical spirit carefully and complete a risk assessment. Elements of this activity are adult only tasks.

Cardboard tube bonfire print

What you need:

- Cardboard tubes
- Scissors
- Paint tray
- Red, yellow and orange paint
- Dark paper

What to do:

1. Snip the cardboard tubes in a series of straight lines from one end, into the middle.

2. Bend the strips back so that they are at 90 degrees to the tube.

3. Carefully cut the ends of the strips into triangular points.

4. Decant a range of coloured paints into the paint tray.

5. Dip the cut end of the tube into the paint, whilst holding onto the uncut end. Try to dip in all the colours.

6. Print the painted end onto the dark paper, to create a bonfire print.

Taking it forward

- Sprinkle the picture with sequins or glitter while the paint is still wet, for additional sparkle!

What's in it for the children?

The children will be able to talk about why they have used 'hot' colours to make their print look like flames. They will also enjoy the printing activity!

Olive investigation

What you need:

- Olive oil
- Water tray, Tuff Spot or bowl
- Olives (different varieties and colours)
- Scoops and spoons
- Clear containers

What to do:

1. Pour the oil into the tray or bowl.
2. Add the olives.
3. Let the children experience the texture and smell of the olives.
4. Give the children the opportunity to pull some of the olives apart to reveal the inner flesh and stone.
5. Encourage the children to fill containers with oil and hold them up to the light.

Taking it forward

- Add other resources to this activity such as candles, which will link the oil to its symbolism for this festival.
- Food colouring can be added for further visual stimulation.

What's in it for the children?

This is a real sensory experience with the texture, smell and possibly also the taste of the olives.

Latke flip

What you need:

- Paint
- Paintbrushes
- Paper plate
- Lolly stick
- Tape or glue
- Card
- Scissors
- Brown paper
- String

What to do:

1. Paint the paper plate and the lolly stick to look like a frying pan.
2. Attach the lolly stick to the paper plate with tape or glue.
3. Cut out a piece of card in the shape of a 'latke'.
4. Cover the card 'latke' in brown paper and stick it in place.
5. Cut a long piece of string.
6. Attach one end of the string to the paper plate and the other to the brown paper 'latke'.
7. Use the paper plate 'frying pan' to flip the 'latke' and catch it again.

Taking it forward

- Why not set up some 'latke' flipping races?
- To make the flipping and catching more challenging, remove the string.

What's in it for the children?

This is a great activity for promoting the development of balance, hand–eye coordination, and fine and gross motor skills.

Glowing oil

What you need:

- Fluorescent paint
- Small bowls
- Olive oil (or baby oil)
- Tray or plate
- Black light or bulb
- Pipettes or droppers
- Cotton buds

What to do:

1. Put the fluorescent paint into the small bowls.
2. Pour the oil into the tray or plate.
3. Switch on the black light.
4. Use the pipettes to draw up the paint and drop it into the oil.
5. Mix and gently move the paint, using the cotton bud, to create patterns.

Taking it forward

- Try this on a much larger scale in a water tray with more oil, and turkey basters as well as pipettes.

What's in it for the children?

This is a brilliant demonstration of how paint reacts when it is mixed with oil. Adults can discuss with the children the importance of oil in the Hanukkah celebrations, and also the symbolism of the glowing light.

Dreidel spinner

What you need:

- Dreidel (or photograhs as examples)
- Felt tips
- Old CDs
- Blu-Tak or modelling clay
- Paper

What to do:

1. Talk to the children about a Dreidel (a four-sided top with different Hebrew characters on it). Show them an actual Dreidel or photographs of one.

2. Push a felt tip into the hole in the middle of a CD.

3. If the felt tips are too thin then stick a piece of Blu-Tak or modelling clay over the hole to help the felt tip stay in position.

4. Place the CD onto the paper.

5. Hold the end of the felt tip and spin the CD.

6. Let the CD spin, making marks as it goes.

7. Encourage the children to repeat until they have created a pattern.

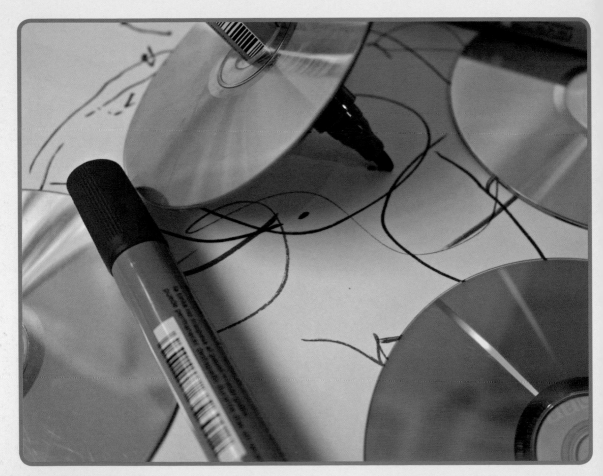

Taking it forward

- Add some Dreidel symbols to the top of the CD.

- Talk to the children about how the CD reflects the light as it spins, and the importance of the symbol of light at Hanukkah.

What's in it for the children?

Making the CD spin can be a bit tricky to begin with, so it is a good activity for helping children to develop their fine motor dexterity. It is also a chance to learn about religious symbols and their meanings.

Snowman slime

What you need:

- 1 bowl
- Wooden spoon for stirring
- 2 cups of PVA glue
- 1½ cups of very warm water
- Essence (if you want it to smell)
- Glitter
- ½ cup of liquid starch or 1½ cups of cornflour
- Any enhancements to make arms, a nose and eyes such as twigs, buttons, pebbles etc!

What to do:

1. Mix the PVA glue, 1½ cups of water, a few drops of essence and some glitter in a bowl.
2. Next, pour in the liquid starch or cornflour.
3. Stir the contents until they are thoroughly blended.
4. Leave to set, until gloopy.
5. Allow the children to experiment with the texture of the slime on a clean surface.
6. Once they have formed their snowman shape they can add decorations to make the arms, nose and eyes.

SKIN allergy!

What's in it for the children?

Children are able to observe the change in the materials as well as experiencing the unique texture of the slime.

 Health & Safety

Make sure this is a closely supervised activity and a risk assessment is in place.

Twig stars

What you need:

- Scissors
- 6 twigs
- Sandwich ties or florist's wire
- Glue
- Glitter (optional)
- Ribbon

What to do:

1. Trim all the twigs to the same length.
2. Make two triangles with the twigs.
3. Secure the points of each triangle with the sandwich ties or wire.
4. Glue the two triangles together to create a twig star.
5. Spread glue over the star and sprinkle with glitter before the glue dries.
6. Leave the whole creation to dry.
7. Once dry, loop the ribbon through one of the triangle points so that the children can hang up their sparkly star decorations!

Taking it forward

- Make one full triangle and leave one corner of the second triangle open. Use this corner to weave the second triangle into the first. Seal the ends with ties or wire.

What's in it for the children?

This is a really simple but effective activity and helps with shape recognition. You can make the stars as big or as little as you like. Depending on the size, they are really good for children's fine and gross motor development.

Snowman shooters

What you need:

- Black paper
- Orange paper
- Scissors
- Glue
- White paper cups
- White balloons
- Pom-poms or white mini marshmallows (to look like mini snowballs)

What to do:

1. Cut features such as eyes, nose, mouth etc. from the coloured papers and stick them on the white paper cup to create a snowman face.
2. Cut off the top third of a balloon.
3. Let the children stretch the bottom two thirds of the balloon over the base of their cup, leaving the mouthpiece hanging down.
4. Put a pom-pom into the snowman cup.
5. Hold the cup firmly.
6. Pull down on the mouthpiece of the balloon.
7. Let go and watch the pom-pom fly!

Taking it forward

- For a fun variation try changing the design of the paper cup to Father Christmas or Rudolph.
- Why not try having a pom-pom catching competition?

What's in it for the children?

This is a good activity for showing children cause and effect as well as helping them to develop their fine motor dexterity.

50 fantastic ideas for celebrations and festivals

Cotton reel Christmas lists

What you need:

- Tape measure
- Cotton reels
- Ruler
- Scissors
- Paper
- Pencils
- Paint and other decorative materials
- Glue

What to do:

1. Measure the width of the outside of the cotton reel.
2. Use the ruler to measure a strip of paper with the same width (how long the paper is will depend on the length of the Christmas list!)
3. Cut out the strip of paper.
4. Draw or write a Christmas list onto the paper.
5. Paint and decorate the cotton reel ends.
6. Carefully glue the end of the list to the cotton reel and wrap the rest of the list around it.

Taking it forward

- Wind thread or string around one end of the cotton reel to make it into a hanging decoration.
- To make it less fiddly, ask children to write their list on a large sheet of paper and use the photocopier to reduce it down.

What's in it for the children?

Children have the opportunity to talk about their likes and dislikes as well as being able to practise their creative and mark making skills.

Snowman window stickers

What you need:

- Several small bowls
- Several mixing spoons
- PVA glue
- **Paint** (powder or ready mixed)
- **Glitter** (optional)
- Greaseproof paper
- **Paintbrushes or squeezy bottle**

What to do:

1. Mix equal parts of PVA glue and paint (as PVA dries clear, the paint will provide the colour).
2. Repeat this step for all of the colours the children might need – for example a snowman sticker would need white, black and orange!
3. If the children are using glitter, add it to the mixtures.
4. Spread flat a sheet of greaseproof paper.
5. Either 'dribble' the mixture onto the paper using a paintbrush, or decant the glue into bottles and squeeze it out into a snowman shape.
6. Use the different colours to add decoration.
7. Leave to dry.
8. Once dry, peel off the paper and stick the PVA snowman onto a window.

Taking it forward

- Make a complete snowman all at once, or for less confident children, make the individual parts and stick them together on the window.
- Use the same process to make a collection of other Christmas characters!

What's in it for the children?

The children will enjoy experimenting with the texture of the glue and paint mixture. They can also observe a change in materials as the glue changes from a liquid to a solid. Focusing on decorating their creations will develop their fine motor dexterity.

Bauble balance

What you need:

- Kitchen roll tube
- Paint (and paintbrushes) or wrapping paper
- Small garden cane
- Timer
- Selection of Christmas baubles

What to do:

1. Decorate the kitchen roll tube with paint or wrapping paper.
2. Stand the tube on its end.
3. Balance a small garden cane along the top of the tube.
4. Turn over the timer.
5. Let the children take turns to balance a bauble on either end of the cane without it falling off!

Taking it forward

- When the children are confident with the task, reduce the time allowed.
- Use different sized and shaped baubles to increase the challenge.

What's in it for the children?

The children will develop their ability to make estimations about weight and balance, as well as working against the clock!

Confetti launcher

What you need:

- Plastic bottles
- Scissors
- Balloons
- Confetti

What to do:

1. Carefully cut the neck and end off the plastic bottle.
2. Place the 'mouth' of the balloon over the neck of the bottle.
3. Turn upside down and pour confetti into the balloon.
4. Holding onto the neck of the bottle, stretch the balloon downwards.
5. Release!

Taking it forward

- Try using different sized bottles and different amounts and types of confetti.

What's in it for the children?

Cutting a bottle can be a challenge for some children, who may require adult support. They will be experiencing cause and effect first hand as they stretch the balloon and then watch it shoot confetti into the air!

 Health & Safety

Watch out for sharp edges when cutting the plastic bottles.

Salad spinner fireworks

What you need:

- Paper
- Scissors
- Salad spinner
- Paint
- Paintbrush or pipette
- Glitter

What to do:

1. Cut some paper into a circle that will fit inside the salad spinner.
2. Place the paper inside the spinner.
3. Use a pipette or paintbrush to drop blobs of paint onto the paper.
4. Put the lid on the salad spinner.
5. Spin the handle, keeping a hand on the lid to stop it from flying off.
6. When the salad spinner has stopped, remove the lid.
7. If the children want to add glitter, add it whilst the paint is wet, then leave the paper to dry.

Taking it forward

- This can be developed into a large scale outdoors activity. Use strong tape to attach string to each corner of a builders tray, hang it from a washing line, add paint and spin!

What's in it for the children?

Alongside some colour mixing, the children are given a demonstration of forces and how they affect the movement of the paint inside the salad spinner.

Time capsule shoebox

What you need:

- Photographs
- Pictures
- Artefacts
- Shoebox
- Felt tips, paint and collage materials
- Paper and pens
- String or tape

What to do:

1. Spend time talking about key events or moments that have happened during the course of the year.

2. Collect a range of photographs, pictures and artefacts that illustrate these moments.

3. Ask the children to personalise the outside of their shoebox to represent the individual or group who are creating it. They could use a variety of craft materials such as felt tips, paint and collage to decorate it.

4. Fill the box with everything that has been collected and then seal it up with a message about its contents.

5. Hide it away in a safe place!

Taking it forward

- Get families involved in putting together a more personal version of a child's time capsule.

What's in it for the children?

This is a great opportunity for children to have time to think about key events that have taken place over the year, remember them in order, and gain a better concept of the passing of time.

50 fantastic ideas for celebrations and festivals

Drinking straw party blower

What you need:

- **Large drinking straw**
- **Scissors**
- **Dinner plate, bowl or saucer** (depending on the size of the party blower)
- **Paper or card**
- **Pencil**
- **Felt tips, sequins and other craft resources**
- **Glue or sellotape**

What to do:

1. Squash one end of the drinking straw.
2. Cut all the corners off the squashed end - there is no exact science to this bit!
3. Use some paper and a pencil to draw around the dinner plate, bowl or saucer, and carefully cut it out.
4. Decorate one side of the paper using craft resources such as felt tips and sequins.
5. Cut a straight line from the edge of the circle into the middle.
6. Fold the edges of the straight line over each other to form a cone, with the decorated side facing outwards.
7. Secure the cone shape with glue or sellotape.
8. Cut off the pointy end of the cone to fit the straw in (the children are going to blow into the straw).
9. Secure the straw with sellotape or glue.
10. Blow to make a lot of noise!

Taking it forward

- Make a huge party blower with a piece of plastic pipe and a funnel. Attach the funnel to one end of the plastic pipe with tape. Put the straw inside the other end of the pipe and blow down the straw. The pipe will amplify the sound, like a makeshift horn!

What's in it for the children?

There are lots of different processes in this activity from the decoration, to the construction. The best thing about it is the amount of noise that it makes!

Memory string

What you need:

- Paper
- Pen
- Photographs
- Felt tips and pencils
- Artefacts
- Hole punch
- Coloured string, wool or thread

What to do:

1. Talk to the children about the key things they remember from the past year.
2. Make a list of what they discuss.
3. Collect photographic evidence, ask the children to draw a picture, or find an artefact related to their memories.
4. Arrange all of these things in chronological order.
5. Use the hole punch and tie them together with the string, wool or thread.
6. Hang them up.
7. Ask the children to talk through their memories.

Taking it forward

- Create a memory string as a whole class or group, as well as an individual.
- Ask parents and carers to create a family memory string at home.

What's in it for the children?

This activity helps children to make sense of, and order their own biography, and to appreciate the concept of time passing.

Chinese jump rope art

CHINESE NEW YEAR

What you need:

- Chinese jump ropes
- Easels
- Tape
- Paper
- Paint
- Trays
- Sponges
- Strong tape

What to do:

1. Loop the Chinese jump rope around the easel and secure at the back with tape.
2. Put paper onto the easel.
3. Decant some paint into the trays.
4. Dip the sponges into the paint.
5. Hold the sponge in the middle of the rope and stretch it away from the easel as far as possible.
6. Let go of the sponge and the rope.
7. Once the sponge has hit the easel, repeat the process until the children are happy with the results.

Taking it forward

- Experiment with different sized sponges and pieces of fabric to achieve different effects.

What's in it for the children?

This activity is great for helping children to develop their gross motor skills, hand-eye coordination, balance and upper body strength, as well as making some experimental art!

Fire breathing dragon

What you need:

- Photographs of a Chinese dragon
- Paper cups
- Scissors
- Red paint
- Paintbrushes
- Felt tips
- Red and orange tissue papers
- Glue

What to do:

1. Explain to the children they are going to make a Chinese dragon and show them photographs to inspire them.

2. Cut a small hole in the bottom of the paper cup.

3. Paint the cup red and leave to dry (or buy red paper cups, if possible).

4. Once dry, use the felt tips to add details so that the cup looks like a Chinese dragon. Make sure that the face is drawn as though the drinking end of the cup is the dragon's mouth.

5. Cut the tissue paper into strips about 20cm long.

6. Stick the strips around the drinking end of the cup.

7. Instruct the children to hold the bottom of the cup up to their mouth and blow through the small hole.

8. The dragons will look like they are breathing fire!

Taking it forward

- Make this on a larger scale by decorating a plant pot in the same way. For a really big dragon, use a bucket and a hairdryer!

What's in it for the children?

This is a good opportunity to discuss one of the main symbols of the Chinese New Year. The children will be able to experiment with controlling the effect of their breath on the tissue paper, and so will learn about cause and effect.

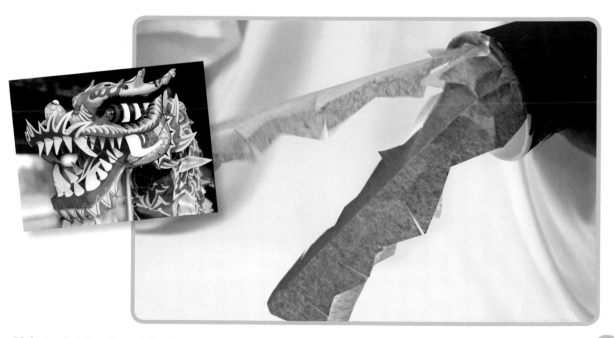

Glow-in-the-dark noodles

What you need:

- Pan
- Tonic water
- Thread noodles
- Access to a hob
- Colander or sieve
- Black light
- Bowls
- Chopsticks

What to do:

1. Fill a pan with tonic water.
2. Add the noodles and cook as per the instructions (adult only).
3. When the noodles are cooked, drain them using the colander.
4. Display in a dark space using a black light, and watch the noodles glow.
5. Encourage the children to explore the texture of the noodles. They could use the chopsticks to help!

Taking it forward

- Add glow-in-the-dark paint to make different colours (see picture). Ensure the children don't eat the coloured noodles!
- Cook these noodles on a larger scale and fill a water tray with them. Encourage the children to explore the texture.

What's in it for the children?

The noodles demonstrate a change in property when they are added to hot water. This is also a good activity to learn how to use chopsticks!

 Health & Safety
Elements of this activity are adult only tasks.

Chopstick drums

What you need:

- Balloons
- Scissors
- Empty tin cans (safely opened)
- Elastic bands
- Craft resources for decoration
- Chopsticks

What to do:

1. Cut the bottom third off the balloon (the bit you blow through).

2. Stretch the remaining top two thirds over the open end of a tin can. Take care with the can edges.

3. Secure the balloon with an elastic band.

4. Decorate the sides of the can with whatever craft materials will inspire the children.

5. Let the children play the handmade Chinese drums using the chopsticks.

Taking it forward

- Make bigger drums, substituting the balloon with fabric or plastic.

What's in it for the children?

The children can enjoy creating rhythm with their drums, as well as learning about Chinese culture and celebration.

Health & Safety

Ensure that there are no sharp edges on the tin cans.

Moon cakes

What you need:

- Access to an oven
- A large mixing bowl
- Wooden spoon for stirring
- ½ cup salted butter
- ¼ cup sugar
- 2 egg yolks
- 1 cup plain flour
- Clingfilm
- Access to a fridge
- A flat, clean surface
- 1 cup strawberry jam (this is instead of the traditional red bean paste)
- Baking tray

What to do:

1. Preheat the oven to 220°C (200°C fan oven).
2. Combine the butter, sugar, 1 egg yolk (reserve the second egg yolk) and stir.
3. Mix in the flour and stir carefully until fully combined.
4. When the dough starts to come together, wrap it in clingfilm and put it in the fridge.
5. Refrigerate the dough for half an hour.
6. Take the dough and roll it into small balls, on a clean surface.
7. Make a hole with your thumb in the centre of each ball.
8. Fill the hole with a teaspoon of jam, and place on a baking tray.
9. Beat the remaining egg yolk and brush each cake with it.
10. Bake for twenty minutes or until the outside edges are golden.
11. Leave to cool - hot jam will burn!

Taking it forward

- Talk to the children about the tradition of making and eating moon cakes.

- Take a look at traditional designs to discuss with the children.

What's in it for the children?

There are lots of processes involved in the preparation and baking of these cakes. Not to mention the sensory pleasure of eating them once they are finished!

➕ **Health & Safety**

The children must be carefully supervised when using the oven.

Bubble jumping

What you need:

- Red and gold wrapping paper
- Strong tape
- Scissors
- Large bubble wrap

What to do:

1. Tape the wrapping paper to the floor.
2. Also tape a length of bubble wrap over the top.
3. Ask the children to remove their shoes and socks.
4. To simulate the noise of firecrackers, children jump up and down on the bubble wrap to burst the bubbles.

Taking it forward

- If there isn't any wrapping paper, colour the back of some of the bubbles with permanent marker and then tape on top of white paper. The wrapping paper could also be replaced with colourful tissue paper.

What's in it for the children?

This is a very physical and noisy activity! The children will be working on their balance and coordination as well as learning about a Chinese custom.

Fire cracker cardboard tubes

What you need:

- One and a half cardboard tubes for each cracker
- Red paint
- Paintbrush
- Small bowl (for the paint)
- Gold or black pen
- Scissors
- Stapler and staples
- Party poppers
- String

What to do:

1. Paint one of the cardboard tubes red and leave to dry.
2. Decorate it with gold or black pen to resemble Chinese writing.
3. Take the other cardboard tube and cut it in half.
4. Squeeze one end of the halved tube and staple it at either side leaving a gap in the middle.
5. Thread the string of the party popper through the hole that has just been created. The party popper should now be sitting inside the halved tube, with its string hanging out of the bottom.
6. Push this half tube inside the painted tube and secure around the top with staples (see picture below).
7. Repeat to make a cracker for every child.
8. Attach some string to the crackers and hang them together in clusters.
9. When everyone is ready to make their cracker go 'bang', pull the string attached to the party popper.
10. To re-use, replace the party popper.

Taking it forward

- Make a simpler version by decorating the cardboard tube, but without the party popper inside.
- Use the firecrackers as part of a Chinese dance or celebration.

What's in it for the children?

The children will have to follow instructions to construct their crackers, as well as enjoying making them go bang!

 Health & Safety

When using party poppers ensure that the children are supervised and the popper is pointing away from children and adults at all times.

fortune cookies

What you need:

- Coloured paper or thin card
- Glass or cup
- Pencil
- Scissors
- Glue

What to do:

1. Write a fortune such as 'Good luck', 'Be happy' on pieces of paper no longer than the width of the glass or cup.

2. Draw around the glass or cup onto another piece of paper or thin card to make a circle.

3. Cut out the circle.

4. Fold in half, but don't crease down the fold.

5. Tuck the fortune inside the folded circle. Make sure that it is folded small enough that it will not touch the edges.

6. Bring the two outside ends of the semi-circle towards the middle.

7. Glue these two ends in place.

8. Ask the children to swap 'fortune cookies' and open them to discover their fortunes!

Taking it forward

- Use patterned paper to make the cookies with.

- Alternatively, use plain paper and ask the children to decorate the paper before they fold it into cookies.

What's in it for the children?

This activity will encourage children to think about others so make sure they write positive messages.

It will also help them to develop their fine motor skills because folding the cookies can be tricky to begin with!

Good luck!

Great happiness

Great fortune!

Good health!

Good luck eggs

What you need:

- Teaspoons
- Eggs
- Container for leftover raw egg
- Hot soapy water
- Confetti, coloured rice, glitter or sequins
- A hoover!

What to do:

1. Use a teaspoon to crack a raw egg as if it were a boiled egg, and take off the top third.

2. Pour out the yolk and white (this can be saved for another project, such as Moon cakes pg 50).

3. Wash out the eggshell in soapy water.

4. Once dry, fill with confetti, coloured rice, glitter or sequins.

5. Children take it in turns to gently 'crack' an egg on the heads of their friends.

6. Explain that the falling confetti is a symbol of good luck and good fortune to come.

Taking it forward

- Add a message of good luck or good fortune into the egg for the recipient to find and read.

- Use a hole punch and some coloured paper to create homemade confetti!

What's in it for the children?

The children can enjoy the surprise of cracking the eggs open! They could also develop their social awareness as they think about others and wish them good fortune.

✚ Health & Safety

Some parts of this activity are adult only tasks.

Crunchy chicks

What you need:

- 3 cups mini marshmallows
- A pan
- Wooden spoon
- Access to a hob
- 3½ cups puffed rice cereal
- A clean, flat surface
- Chocolate chips
- Sweets for decoration

What to do:

1. Slowly melt the marshmallows in a pan (adult only).
2. Add the puffed rice to the marshmallows and carefully stir in.
3. Leave to cool, but not until it is completely set.
4. When cool enough to touch, roll several ball shapes in two different sizes (one for the head and one for the body).
5. Decorate the head with chocolate chips for the eyes and sweets for the beak.
6. Place some sweets on the body to make wings.
7. Leave to cool, then let the children enjoy eating their creations!

Taking it forward

- Create a nest for the chicks to sit in out of melted chocolate and shredded wheat!
- Use orange peel as an extra sensory element to create a beak and wings (see picture).

What's in it for the children?

Children will also use their fine motor dexterity to model the chicks.

 Health & Safety

Melting the ingredients is a task for adults only, or must be closely supervised.

Conker eggs

What you need:

- Eggs
- Pan
- Water
- Access to a hob
- Felt tips

Taking it forward

- To make the game more challenging introduce some extra rules about how to hold the egg, or where to stand.

What to do:

1. Place the eggs in a pan and hard-boil them – this should take roughly 10 minutes (adult only).

2. Carefully drain the pan and fill with cold water to help the eggs to cool.

3. Leave the eggs until they are cold.

4. Let the children decorate them with felt tips.

5. Take it in turns to hold an egg and use it to try and crack an opponents' egg (small ends together, see picture below).

6. The winning egg goes on to the next round!

What's in it for the children?

The children will have to use what they know about eggs to try and make sure that theirs doesn't break. There is also a child whose egg will get smashed every time. This helps them to enjoy the playing of the game and build resilience!

✚ Health & Safety
Elements of this activity are adult only tasks.

Dragon Easter eggs

What you need:

- 6 eggs
- Pan
- Water
- Access to a hob
- Food colouring
- Small bowls, containers or plastic bag
- Spoon
- Clean, hard surface

What to do:

1. Hard-boil the eggs in a pan of water (adult only). This should take approximately ten minutes.

2. Carefully drain the pan and fill with cold water to help the eggs to cool.

3. Leave the eggs until they are cold.

4. While the eggs are cooling, mix a strong solution of food colouring and water in the small bowls, containers or a plastic bag. There needs to be enough liquid to completely cover an egg.

5. Once cooled, roll the eggs on a hard surface whilst applying a little pressure, to crack the shell all over the egg. Do not remove the shells.

6. Submerge the cracked eggs in the bowls of coloured liquid and leave overnight.

7. Remove from the liquid, rinse, and then remove the shell to reveal a wonderful coloured pattern.

Taking it forward

- Try covering only half of the egg in liquid, and then repeat the process using a different colour on the other blank half of the egg.

- Eat the dragon's eggs for a snack!

What's in it for the children?

This is an opportunity to discuss how the heat has changed the egg from a liquid to a solid, and also how cracking the shell has allowed the colour to dye parts of the egg.

✚ Health & Safety

Elements of this activity are adult only tasks.

Egg splat and roll!

What you need:

- Tray
- Paper
- **Plastic eggs** (with holes in the end)
- **Ready mixed paint, in a range of colours**

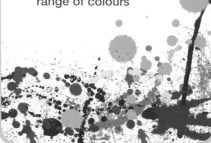

What to do:

1. Cover the bottom of a tray with paper.
2. Fill the plastic eggs with different coloured paints.
3. Choose two or three eggs.
4. Drop them into the tray.
5. Roll the eggs around the tray to distribute the paint. Ask the children to work on making a pattern using this technique.

Taking it forward

- Use a large builders' tray so that a number of children can work together.

- Try using the empty eggshells from boiled eggs. Fill with paint and then drop them from a height to create a great splat picture!

What's in it for the children?

The children will enjoy colour mixing as well as gross motor, balance and dexterity development.

Shaving foam eggs

What you need:

- Plastic tray or glass casserole dish
- Shaving foam
- Food colouring
- Cotton buds
- **Eggs** (the lighter in colour, the better)
- Rubber gloves
- Kitchen roll

What to do:

1. Cover the bottom of a tray or dish with shaving foam (it doesn't have to be deep).
2. Dot some food colouring at various points across the shaving foam.
3. Use a cotton bud to swirl the food colouring through the foam.
4. Place an egg at one side of the tray and roll it carefully across the tray. This is easiest when the children gently tip the tray.
5. Using rubber gloves, lift the egg out and leave to dry for around ten minutes.
6. Once dry wipe the excess foam off the egg with a piece of kitchen roll.

Taking it forward

- As well as creating single colour eggs, experiment with a range of colours to make multi-coloured eggs.
- Add beads, sequins, glitter, and other decorative materials to the finished egg to make it even more spectacular!

What's in it for the children?

This is a chance to experiment with colour mixing and dying as well as perfecting the tricky art of trying to make an egg roll in a straight line!

bubble wrap eggstravaganza

What you need:

- Brown paper
- Ironing board
- Bubble wrap
- Craft resources such as sequins, feathers, buttons, glitter
- Iron
- Scissors

Taking it forward

- Use bubble wrap with different sized bubbles for a different effect.
- Include the children's drawings inside a bubble wrap Easter egg.

What's in it for the children?

This activity demonstrates how heat can change and transform the properties of some objects.

What to do:

1. Put a piece of brown paper onto the ironing board.
2. Lay a smaller piece of bubble wrap on top of the brown paper with the bubbles facing up.
3. On top of the bubble wrap place lots of craft resources such as sequins, feathers, buttons, glitter, and any other materials that will inspire the children!
4. Now lay a second piece of bubble wrap on top of the first, this time with the bubbles facing down.
5. Lay a second piece of brown paper on top of the whole thing.
6. Using a hot iron (adult only), iron over the bubble wrap, through the brown paper.
7. Remove the brown paper to find that the two pieces of bubble wrap have fused together, trapping all of the objects in the middle.
8. Carefully cut into an egg shape.

Health & Safety

Elements of this activity are adult only tasks. Ensure that a risk assessment is in place.

Onion skin eggs

What you need:

- The skin of 10 brown onions
- Stainless steel pan
- 4½ cups of water
- 2 tablespoons of white vinegar
- Access to a hob
- Sieve
- Leaf, ribbon or string
- Uncooked eggs (still in their shells)
- Several pairs of nude or tan coloured tights
- Slotted spoon

What to do:

1. Put the onion skins into the pan.
2. Add the water and the vinegar.
3. Place on the hob, bring to the boil and simmer for twenty minutes (adult only).
4. Use the sieve to strain the onion skins. Reserve the strained water for the next step.
5. Wrap a leaf, ribbon or string around an egg and hold it in place by wrapping the egg in the foot of a pair of tights. Chop the tights so that there is enough left to knot, then tightly knot the open end.
6. Put the eggs into the coloured onion water and simmer for up to twenty minutes.
7. Lift out with a slotted spoon and leave to cool.

What's in it for the children?

The children will have to follow instructions, observe the process that is taking place, and also see how heat can produce a permanent change in an object.

Health & Safety

Elements of this activity are adult only tasks. Ensure that a risk assessment is in place.